Religion or Relationship

Religion or Relationship

Living with the Holy Spirit

Patricia Rowe Mitola

ReadersMagnet, LLC

Religion or Relationship: Living with the Holy Spirit

Published in the United States of America
ISBN Paperback: 978-1-952896-33-0
ISBN eBook: 978-1-952896-34-7

ReadersMagnet, LLC
10620 Treena Street, Suite 230 | San Diego, California, 92131 USA
1.619.354.2643 | www.readersmagnet.com

Cover design by Ericka Obando
Interior design by Shemaryl Tampus

Table of Contents

Prologue

A New Beginning
March 2017

THE PURPOSE OF THIS HOOK is to clarify your walk with God and to build you up to the faith that we speak and the desire is to guide your studies of God's Word toward a real relationship and not just works or activities, and toward being led by the Spirit of God.

So, pray—take a deep breath and hang on as we discuss this most important issue. John 8:32 "…and you will know the truth and the truth will make you free." Hopefully, this discussion will help you be free to enjoy His presence in your life. The examples provided are only a few, but the relationship continues day by day.

Words… words… words. Our culture has become so loose and careless in conversation and in everyday life that you may say anything you want, any way you want, to try to communicate what it is you want to communicate depending upon how you feel at the moment. Then, over time, words lose their true meanings because we have lost the importance of honesty and truth for the sake of pleasing ourselves. This carries over into the way we read the Bible. We choose to accept what we think or what we want the Word to say as though it is just another person who is saying those words. With each generation, it becomes easier to read, lay the Bible aside, and try to recall what was said, or the purpose of it, and what it meant to us from God. The influence of our language is seriously affected by how seriously we follow television and other modern-day communication devices. Society has become very casual and not serious, which is fine, but there are times to be serious, protective, and correct for important reasons. It is OK to say what you mean, mean what you say, and more importantly to know what you believe, live as you believe it, and claim the truth.

Parents are encouraged to be less disciplinary, but to encourage pleasure, fun, and happiness with limited negative results. That casts shadows over a disciplined parent, plus elicits further negative responses when children get into school with other children and/or teachers who now think the correction is unhealthy for the child.

The next step is how to balance the opposites. Gradually the children have to decide how they should behave depending upon where they are and who is in charge. So the trend grows to where we are today. Where does life with the Lord fit? The decision comes down to, "Who is God? Do I believe Him, or believe in Him? When should I follow Him, even if or when I read His Word? Do I continue believing and following God when I am in or out of church if I go, or if my parents are around? When I grow up, what decisions will I make about how to live my life?" The list goes and grows. People who grow up in a Christian faith either continue practicing the life-style or leave it. They may marry someone who has some of the same beliefs and practices, or someone who has none at all. Then it is a matter of, "How do we raise our children—or let someone else teach them?" Then maybe they will grow very differently from their family. This all began and grew because we play with words, either intentionally or without knowledge or intent. How do we recover from the careless influences and understand the importance of the words of the Bible compared to all other words we hear and use everywhere else?

God does not play with words. He means what He says and teaches truth from His viewpoint. He is God and He created the world, knows all things, can control all things, it makes sense to believe His words. Read the Bible; learn what is true and how He has prepared a place for us and tells us in John 14:2 that He will come again to take us to be with Him. That is what He means, but we must know that if we are going to be with Him, we need to belong to Him and be in His family by our desire and choice. He does not need to beg or force, but it should be only by our choice.

This is where good communication and understanding come in so we can be in heaven for eternity with Him. It is all in the Bible: how we can be received by Him and live for Him in this world. It is a common problem to trust who is teaching us. However, if we have not been taught but are educated, we can read for ourselves, listen to teachers, and study if we care enough to acknowledge the truth when we find it. Then it is up to us to learn all the truth, stand on it, live it, teach it on God's opinion—not just anyone! The study, ask questions and as the Bible teaches, invite Jesus to come into your heart and life to take your sins away and to be your Lord and Savior. The Bible considered religious information is given to us by God himself so we can be with Him when we die. These are important issues: 1. In the beginning was God; 2. The truths about creation; 3. The Ten Commandments; 4. Learning studying, growing; 5. Believe Jesus died on the cross for you; 6. Develop a study and prayer life and relationship with God after you have accepted Him.

These may seem repetitious, but are basic expectations from God and must be emphasized. Does everyone worship the same? Many probably do, but we only get to heaven on an individual basis, by personal choice, by believing who He is and what He has done for us. Now here is the most important issue. Does all this believing the above information, regularly attending prescribed services, fulfilling prescribed responsibilities and saying prescribed prayers at given times get you to heaven? All these issues are about believing information, attending services, etc., fulfilling prescribed kinds of behavior and are called a religion, or being religious by identification, Jesus said, "1 am the way the truth and the life. No man cometh to the Father but by Me" (John 14:6). Even believing all those words does not get you to heaven unless you believe and act and choose to have that relationship with Him-your choice plus nothing else. The relationship is not only on Sunday. You choose to live with His presence in you. Unfortunately, a lot of people think if you keep the routine, it is the same thing. How often do you talk to your best friend? Believing all the facts and other knowledge does not change you any more than knowing everything about a car and how it works makes you a car. You must follow Him and be willing to let Him in charge of your life for His purposes. Then you grow up in Him and build the relationship; then He does become your best friend and you share all your interests with Him more and more. Then beginning regular prayer and Bible study helps you grow in knowing Him more and builds the relationship. The more time you spend with your Friend, the better you know Him. John 15 gives a great illustration of that. Then we can begin to bear fruit. This choice is up to you. This is the day—maybe this very hour—for you to grow in His truth and grace. Hopefully, the stories will help you to understand how to grow in His presence. May God bless you!

Introduction

Insights and Incites

Introduction and Exhortation

THIS BOOK IS FOR ANYONE who truly desires to live in submission to the One and Only Creator, Our Lord, who created this world and who is in total control. He is our provider and protector and our director in as much as we choose Him to be in our lives. When we understand who He is and desires for Him to be in control, then He will continue to live in us by His Holy Spirit and use our lives for whatever purpose He made us accomplish. Jesus tells us, in the gospel of John chapters 14-16, that He came to earth to help us understand who He is and what He desires for us. He came to give us a visual example of His truth so we can learn, listen, and follow Him. Then He said He was going to go away, but would not leave us alone; He would send us a helper—a comforter—to live in us and to continue His purpose of leading us to complete His work and purpose for us.

Words mean something-I F-we truly listen and willingly follow we have His direction, with His presence and power in our lives. The key is-do we believe and desire what we say? We must believe who He is and He chooses to come into our lives and save us, which is the reason He came and died on the cross. Then we give our life to Him to complete the work He came into this world to complete because He was going back to heaven. I know this is repetitious, but I hope I completed it well enough because it makes all the difference: it is not just words.

This book provides some examples of how this real God has worked in one life, and how He will work in any surrendered life to guide and protect you and lead you in ways to serve Him and complete His purposes as you go through this life on earth. He has been with me through a variety of circumstances and has faithfully brought me through many changes, losses, heartaches, and concerns, to the best endings. Read these words from John 14-16 and discipline yourself to make serious choices: John 14:21, "He who HAS My commandments and KEEPS them is one who loves Me and he who loves Me will be loved by My Father, and I will love him and disclose Myself to him-John 14:21. It is essential that these truths be known, believed, desired, and lived as your personal choice. The talk is cheap! The Lord does not play around with words as is so common in this world. These words are written in many of the scriptures, which you will see as you read -and IF you read the Bible to see how He wants us to live. I can say this to you because I have lived a long life and learned from experience.

Is this not what your parents taught you while you were growing up—how to behave, how to obey, what kind of person to be, how to treat people, what kind of person to be? They taught you how to respond in situations and what to say, either by words or by how you saw them respond in all those situations. That is what parents do. Well, God is our Heavenly Father and He does that for us through His word: the book of Proverbs is great for that. Actions of other Christians or through His presence in us, and being under His control are all ways He teaches us. That is what the relationship to our Heavenly Father is to be from the beginning of our rebirth to His family.

We must be careful not to allow His teachings in the Bible to only remain as words, but instead see them as instructions from our Father. As we grow in the Lord, the training should become a way of life IF we love Him and obey. This is what can happen if we only have a religion and not a relationship. The knowledge must become our behavior—a change of who we are in Him. If it becomes a belief in knowledge and works, a religion to name and claim only, it will gradually die out and become a routine instead of who you are in Christ.

As you build this relationship, the Lord will be more and more an ever-present guide and protector, as you may be able to see in the examples I have shared, and one day your life will belong to Him first. That is where you will want to be as the relationship becomes richer and more wonderful, with His presence guiding in all areas of your life. This joy and peace has been and is my experience with the Lord today and will be for the rest of my life. It can be the same for you according to your choices.

I trust that through all the repetitions, you will have a desire to a full surrender to the Lord. Again I encourage you to read John chapters 14-16, Romans 8, at least for a complete understanding of who it is waiting for you to come home to your Father for a blessed life.

Hopefully, you will enjoy the examples of how the Lord can and will work in your life as He has in mine, which He has done far more than I have shared, and have a clearer awareness of His presence. He can and will do the same for you. God bless you in the surrender.

Stories

Times when the Lord "Showed up"

God Spoke To Me!

IN AUGUST OF 1955, I went with my cousin to visit my future mother-in-law and father-in-law. Their son and I had gotten engaged shortly before, and I wanted to see them before I went back to college. My future husband was in the Navy. We had a wonderful get-acquainted visit. After a bit, they showed concerns for my religious beliefs, and in the discussion my mother-in-law-to-be asked me if I knew if I would go to heaven ' when I died. I answered, "I believe in the Bible and about Jesus, but I did not know that you could know that. I try to live what the Bible says." They began to encourage us and told us that if we asked Jesus to come into our hearts and asked Him to forgive our sins then He would save us and we would receive eternal life. Soon after the discussion, my cousin and I went home. We did not discuss it any further, but soon after that, we shared that after each of us got home, we individually invited Jesus to come into our hearts and were saved. I began to go to church services at my in-laws' church and enjoyed it.

In October when I came home from school, I was baptized by immersion. I remember so clearly as I was brought up out of the water, I envisioned myself in my suit rising to a stand but saw my body lying in the baptism tank as though I was left there. When I returned to Illinois State University, I began to go to a small Baptist church just off-campus. It was a little green church and was warm and friendly, as was the pastor.

One Sunday morning, the pastor spoke on the subject of living for Jesus and compared it to mountain climbing. He said that each day that we go higher we drive in a new stake and keep going higher. Then he asked, "What stake will you drive in for the Lord Jesus Christ today as you leave the world behind?" This was all new to me. I wanted to please God and thought, "I wonder what God would have me to do?" Immediately into my mind came "lipstick." Well, there was no mentioning of that in the message, or any religion that I knew of that was against lipstick. But since it came to me without any provocation, I had to believe that the message came from God. So I agreed and decided not to wear lipstick anymore.

On the way back to campus, I asked my friends about it and they said they would pray with me about it. When I got back to my room I talked with my roommate who was a Christian. She just listened and said that surely God would not be mad if I just wore a little because I looked a bit pale. So I began to listen to her and wear a little, but then my lips began to crack and bleed, which had never happened to me ever before. This condition did not stop until I decided to quit wearing the lip-stick. So I had to believe that it was God who had spoken to me. So I chose to do away with the lipstick. I heard no more, but I know in my heart it had to be the Lord who spoke to me. and that is fine with me. I believe that God used it to protect me or for my good in His wisdom, and I am as thankful for His interest in me as His child. Ever since I have not and do not wear lipstick.

Testimony of God's Protection

September 1962-1963

FARIBAULT STATE SCHOOL AND HOSPITAL: my first full-time job as a full-time teacher of special children.

It was my first full-time teaching position in the area of my educational studies and a master's degree. I would be working with the mentally disabled in an institutional setting. We had just moved to our home after my husband had completed his Bible studies. I was hired to teach and to begin a special program in physical education. Because of the death of one of the elderly classroom teachers, I was asked to take her place until they could get a replacement. I was young and so excited to be beginning a new and secure level in our lives. I was in my late twenties and a fairly new Christian, having been saved in 1955. My spiritual life was solid in reading Scripture and living it the best I could along with attending a solid Baptist church. Our lives were separated to God and dedicated to His service. Then it happened: my first face-on experience with spiritual warfare.

One of my responsibilities was to every school day walk across campus from the school to the residence area and bring the students who were waiting for me over to the school. There were usually a dozen or so waiting for me. This day there was an extra girl whom I had just met the week before. This girl had taken an unusual dislike for me from the first moment we were introduced. She was seventeen years old, bigger than I, very strong, and had earned her leadership among the girls by her controlling ways. She was also mentally brighter than any of the other girls. They feared her. She had promised me, "I am going to beat you up and get your job." I did not know her, or her capabilities, but I knew she was serious when she first said what she did. Her potential was obvious and my lack of experience at the hospital did not help, but I did not expect her to remember her promise or to be so serious about it.

As I left the school door to get the girls the chanting began. I heard, "P-U Davis, P-U Davis!" loudly across the campus as she led them. The fear took over as the chanting grew louder and I got closer. It rang in my ears as I got closer, and I realized how alone I was. Fear began to set in very strongly, and the weaker I became.

I began to pray, "Lord Jesus, Help me! I don't know what to do! I'm afraid!" I had almost reached the girls, and as I reached them, I looked at Sandy, smiled and greeted her. Immediately she fell to the ground rolling in a grand mal seizure. The aides from the residence ran out, picked her up and carried her into the building to residential care. The rest of the girls followed me as I was instructed to go without her. The Lord had come to my rescue as plain as could be as life itself. Praise be to God! Surely what I saw was spiritual warfare, and the Spirit of God protected me from the evil spirit in her at the very moment I needed Him. Praise His name; this was my introduction to the active spirit world.

She came to my class one more time, and one of the teachers who had been there a long time warned her to go to class and sit down and behave. Sandy turned around to run out of the building. The teacher grabbed her shirt to stop her and it ripped off her as she continued out of the building. I never saw her again. Jesus Christ was the victor and truly protected me, His child. Praise the Lord.

God Is On Time -with Answers

August 1978–1979

In late 1979 I moved to Rhode Island and was hired by the Groden Center, a school for autistic individuals. My responsibilities were to direct the program for teenage and young adults who were autistic. I had responsibilities over two other teachers who each had students to care for, as well as the one student whom I cared for in training. My experiences in training emotionally disturbed students were long and varied in age and types of handicaps, but I had not dealt with autistic students specifically.

My student, Robbie, was a sixteen-year-old young man who could not talk. He became frustrated when he needed to or wanted to communicate a need or desire or interest. He would get excited and scream or sometimes jump up and down in frustration or excitement when trying to communicate.

The initial program for a new student was very specific with the effort to teach them how to understand and communicate basic instruction, such as stand up or sit down. We also covered personal needs communication. We spent each day training students to understand as many words as we could. Robbie was very cooperative and a pleasure to deal with. His home life was frustrating because his father was emotionally not able to cope with Robbie's handicap and disabilities; so he was enrolled in our center. His progress was slow, but he seemed to be intellectually more capable than his progress indicated.

Each week we would have a staff meeting to discuss student progress, problems, and other issues. After working with Robbie in the basic program for a while, at one of the meetings I was asked how things were going. A short report was given, and his slow progress was briefly described and then the meeting opened for discussion. The director asked me what I thought and asked for input. I thought for a moment and out of my mouth came, "How about trying sign language?" He was visually alert but did not seem to understand verbal instruction, as basic as it was. She gave her approval and I made plans to begin.

Several months before I had started to take a sign language class, I had purchased a book already, so even though I was a beginner myself, I had all I needed to help Robbie.

Because he was very visual, he picked up quickly what he had to do. I would show him a sign, demonstrate, and then have him do the same thing. He needed to understand that the sign I gave him was a direction or communication for him. After a couple of times, he got it. From that point his progress was easy and his memory brought him such positives that he moved ahead very quickly and his joy was obvious. On one occasion I was walking through the building with him, he was following. We walked past a shirt hanging in the hall and Robbie reached out with his fingers, touched the sleeve of the shirt and signed "red." He had by then learned his colors and was able to communicate them correctly. He just continued to grow in excitement and the ability to communicate.

At our staff meeting, this progress was shared and the staff was amazed, knowing Robbie. Our director shared this with the education director for the district, and she could not believe it. So we did videotape the class with him and she saw it for herself. There was much joy and excitement because this meant we had another means to be used to educate the handicapped by using sign language. Many avenues were opened. His home life was much improved over time.

This was a result of the good Lord leading me to take sign language class a year before I ever needed it. We have a great God!

I was led that way because the summer before I took a job finding people who would receive a summons. As I was delivering a summons to one place, I rang the doorbell and there was no noise, but as I rang again I noticed a light flashed. Before long a lady came to the door and she let me know that she could not understand me. I had to show her the summons and write basics to her so she could receive the paper.

I could see the importance of basic communication—the reason for taking the class for learning sign language. "God works in wondrous ways His wonders to perform." So I was prepared to help Robbie at my new job that God knew all about a year later. Praise God! Only God knew my future.

Another New Beginning

1979–1980

MANY CHANGES—TOTALLY UNEXPECTED—JUST CAME INTO my life. I knew I would have a job in the fall in another state. What I did not know was that I would lose my home, my car, and my family. All I had was my monthly check from my yearly teaching salary from my job that was divided up into twelve monthly payments until the next school year. The Lord had led me to move our family out of state for a new job, which He provided, and the contract would begin the next coming school year. He had provided a place to stay temporarily, and a car to replace the one I gave to my son who was in college. As soon as school started I could then pay for my other car. There was no extra cash on hand, no savings or checking accounts or charge card. The place for me to live became available soon but I had no money for the down payment, which was required. One day I spoke with an elderly church friend who had discipled me and she asked how much money I had. I told her truthfully that I had ten dollars. She said, "What are you worried about?" I listened and accepted and trusted the Lord. He was all I had, but I was never in a spot like that before. Very soon after that week, I received a check in the mail from my former school district. They had decided to send me my final check early. I had no idea why, but it was right on time and I would be getting paid next from my new job. Praise the Lord! It was right on time and I was able to get the apartment and become settled soon after.

When difficulties come, God is there to protect and provide in as much as we ask Him, depend upon His leading and trust Him. We must honor and respect our Lord and He will be there when we are where He wants us to be when He wants us to be and doing what He has for us to do.

Later on, after I had settled in at my new job, getting paid, and used to my new life, I received a letter from my former school district where I taught before. They informed me that if I could come and substitute in the high school for three days, that would qualify me to fulfill a ten-year period of teaching time there and then I would qualify for retirement when I reached retirement age. Retirement was a rather new thing and I had no idea what a move at that time would do and never even thought about it. What a blessing. It was a blessing to have them do that for me and I know they appreciated my time there. So I called my daughter who lived there and we arranged for me to stay with her and her family while I subbed for the three days. How God provides! We had a chance to visit and I played with my grandchildren and taught school for three days and came home. The Lord had provided a retirement for me that I had earned and could receive one day. I would never have even thought to do that for myself.

When we belong to God through the sacrifices of the Lord Jesus Christ, we are His and He is our caretaker and is faithful to look out for us. This was the beginning of a closer walk with my faithful God. Matthew 6:33 had always been my favorite verse, and now I could add it to a new way of life: “A closer walk with my LORD- a relationship, through His Holy Spirit” (Romans 12:1,2).

God Went Shopping with Me

1980-1981

ONE DAY AFTER I HAD lived in Rhode Island for a while, I was on my way home and remembered I needed something to wear for an occasion. I stopped off at a Target store to see what I could find. I am not a shopper so I asked the Lord, "Please help me to find something that would work and not cost a lot of money- something casual, but nice." As I walked into the store, I noticed the ladies' clothing was down a long aisle and way in the back.

I looked through the dresses and found nothing, so I went to the blouses and behind a short wall there was more to look at, and there I found a blouse striped in pastel colors, pink, yellow, and blue-green. It was very bright cotton and enjoyable to my eyes. I turned it around and checked it out: three-quarter-length sleeves and cut tailoring in the back. I loved it, but thought, "I'm never going to find anything to go with it. Maybe I'll just pick out one color and try to match it." I was thinking about earrings. I always like to match my earrings to go with my clothes. Well, I decided to get the blouse and it was on sale -reduced, and started to buy it. On the way out I thought I would go by the jewelry department just in case, but I had no confidence in getting anything. Near the aisle toward the front of the door was a little table with a whole pile of earrings dumped on it, not on cards or paired. I thought I would take a look out of curiosity. Would you believe I saw one earring in the pile that had not just one color but all three colors that were in that blouse? It also had the same striped pattern as in the blouse. I looked through the pile and found the other one. They matched the blouse so perfectly that I picked them up and put them down a few times just to make sure I did not believe my eyes.

Everywhere I wear them; people ask me if they were a set or how I ever matched them up. It is always an opportunity for me to praise God one more time as I get another chance to tell the story of how God did this for me. He worked that out to bless me for consulting Him for everything in my life! People may think that it is crazy to bother God about those kinds of things, but my God is my personal friend and Father. He is as close as you allow Him to be in everything you allow Him to be and do in your life. It is always a joy to wear that blouse and earrings because God did exactly as I asked Him to do for me and more by teaching me how close He is to me and the degree of His interest in me. He is wonderful and can do anything. It is a great testimony of His love when people ask me how I matched the earrings with the blouse, especially when they know they were not a set. I just let them know, "God my Father did it!"

The Lord Heals All Our Distresses

THE LORD HAD PROVIDED A home for me in Pennsylvania near my son and family, I had not prayed about it, but it seemed that it was the reasonable thing to do. The home was an old schoolhouse close to the church that eventually would call me to minister to their ladies whom the Lord knew, but I had no idea. The home was near my children which helped since my husband's recent death. We were all in agreement that it would be the right thing to do. An old schoolhouse had come up for sale across the field from my son's house. It was reasonable so I bought it and moved. After just a bit of minor reconstruction, it was a great place for a former school teacher. It worked well, for we had always had a compatible relationship. I had always desired to go to a writer's conference and one day a phone call came from a stranger to me, and we had an unplanned conversation. The woman said, "I will be going to a writer's conference -etc, etc,- to which I responded and which ultimately led to my being invited to go along. Since it would be during the coming weekend I had to let my son know because we all went to church together." As a result, of the conference and acquaintances, I was led to a small country church-a bible preaching church-another solid preacher with a positive atmosphere and was asked what my gifts were. I told him that I was a teacher and had taught Bible classes, and done soul winning and one- on- one discipleship. He never said anything else but evidently, this was the place where the Lord wanted me to be. Big change.

He announced soon after on a Sunday morning that I would be teaching a ladies class that would meet downstairs and he would teach the men upstairs. I was thrilled. It worked so well and some of the ladies desired discipleship. It was a bit inconvenient for them because I was not as near to the church as I needed to be. Soon the Pastor said that it would be better for everyone if I lived closer. After prayer, the Lord provided a nice home near the church with a lovely yard at a great price-just what I had talked to the Lord about. So for the good of the Lord's work, and the ministry, which God had given me, the fellowship moved me nearer to my church with little effort and I loved it and the ministry. God blessed the ministry wonderfully.

What a blessing, just short of an acre,2 small storage buildings, clotheslines, a line of fruit trees and birdhouses, I could easily mow the grass-made just to my needs and taste. There were great neighbors on both sides, and handy to the church and ministry. There was a swing on my back porch where I could sit and watch the birds, and all at a reduced price. When we allow our LORD to be first, He is faithful to bless us and provide every need and help us through our trials.

The Lord had truly blessed me and healed my troubles. That little church had become my church home. There was no discussion or questions. That was the first I had heard about the decision. What a blessing to me. God has given me a gift of teaching and I loved doing that. I was so blessed. There were a large number of family-related ladies and a mixture of singles and friends- all seemed to be well acquainted- which was not true, but they accepted me anyway. When we had our first class meeting, I was asked to give my testimony— Pastor told me to just go in there and give my testimony and teach as needed. He knew the acceptance was not sealed--I did not. The class was large for a small church and all were very attentive to me. I gave my story as well as the lesson during complete silence and when I finished, I asked if someone would pray and close the class time. Silence—waiting. Then quietly- sweetly an elderly voice began to pray, thanking God for the message and in chosen words my acceptance. When I saw the Pastor between services, he asked me what happened and how it went. I told him and he asked me who prayed. Little did I know, but the eldest grandma-the basic family of the church was the one who prayed -which meant that I could be accepted. The pastor said, "Good, that meant that you are in and all were agreed if she accepted you". It was a blessed experience and eventually, I became the leader of the ladies' social group. It was one of the most pleasant and blessed years of my life.

One of the ladies-one of THE family had many health issues. She needed treatments regularly along with other problems. She became seriously ill and went to hospital. After a lengthy stay, the doctor said he could do no more to help her, she was going to die. I received the phone call that she was not going to make it. They had to remove all the tubes and support systems. When I went to church that Sunday, I was preparing my classroom and a sister-in-law to her who was in the kitchen told me the situation. Jane was going to die and the kids were already going to her house and taking things out-and on and on. The tone was not what I could accept, so when I got home from church I gave Jane a call at the hospital. She confirmed the news. I asked her, "Jane the Lord is able, what do you want?"

She thought about it for a minute and then said, "I'd like to live long enough to see my children saved."

"Then that is what I am going to ask God to do for you." "Lord, You heard Jane's 'heart desire and I ask, Lord, that if it pleases You, please give her life to see their salvation". Praise the LORD, she did recover and lived a long time-years later. God is so faithful —and the family had to fix a few things. Praise the LORD.

Dominion Over God's Creation

PSALM 8:6-8 2002

One beautiful day, I had my devotions. Usually, I read one chapter in the Psalms, one in the Proverbs, and day by day one chapter in the Old Testament and New Testament beginning in Genesis and going through. Afterward, I decided to take a walkout to the backyard and as I did, I saw at the end of a row of trees a swarm of bees around the last fruit tree at the end of the row. They were very busy and surrounding the tree. I am quite allergic to bee stings, so I decided I had better get the can of spray and get rid of them. I went to get the spray and came out, and as I was walking with the spray can toward the trees, out of the swarm of bees one bee broke away and headed toward me in a straight line. As the bee approached me, I dropped the spray can in fear and pointed at the bee and said, "I claim dominion over you in the name of Jesus!" Immediately, the bee quickly turned back toward the tree and pleasantly flew in a leisurely waving style back to the tree from which he came. God's Word is true again as I praised the Lord, remembering what I had just read a few days ago as I read His Word. God had just said, "You make him rule over the works of Your hands. "You have put all things under his feet, all sheep, and oxen, and also beasts of the field, the birds of the heavens and the fish of the sea, whatever passes through the paths of the seas," 0 Lord, our LORD, how majestic is Your name in all the earth!" Psalm 8:6-8

Once again the LORD showed up and took care of me. Who could doubt why that bee left its mission and returned to its place. I stood there praising God for showing me His presence and protection, as well as His dominion over all creation, by believing Him and who He is.

Time To Go Back Home

IT HAD BEEN MANY YEARS since I moved to Pennsylvania. When my husband died, I believed it was the right time to move near my son and family. I would be buried in Rhode Island where the family burial plot was located, and that is what my husband had requested. So since the aging process was setting in, I thought it was a good time for me to go back. I had learned to ask the Lord what His plans were for me because He is in charge of my life. So I asked the Lord that if it was His will for me to move back to Rhode Island that He would find me an apartment or a place for me to live near my family there.

Before I had left, I knew I would be back, so I placed an application in several senior residences where I could make my home. I called all of them to see if there were any openings. Every one of them said the same thing: "We have nothing available at this time, and it will be several months before we will have anything." So I decided to leave it and try again later. That was on a Thursday. On Monday I received notice that the Shalom Apartments had an opening for me. So I believed that was my answer and God's leading.

Right away I accepted the offer and called my family to see when they could come to get me. My daughter put the phone down when I called and went to see when my grandson could come to move me back to Rhode Island. He could not do it that weekend but would do it the next weekend. Arrangements were set, but my grandson wanted to see if the apartment was acceptable. He was concerned about the nearness of Rt. 95 visually from my window, as well as the large tower outside the end of the building. Since I had asked the Lord to get me a place, and this was the one that came available immediately, I accepted it as from the Lord and they came to get me the next weekend. It meets all my needs, and I am certain that this is where the Lord wants me to be. Who am I to question my Lord's judgment for what I need? Praise the Lord. They moved me in the next weekend as planned, and I followed the Lord's leading to move me back to Rhode Island. I am in the best place to be: in the Lord's will.

Holy Spirit Guidance and Blessing

August 16, 2013

Since May, my life had been made miserable from my wrong choices on the computer, and a scam sent me on a trip changing my name, phone, license and a dozen more ways to get my identity out of the hands of crooks. This could tempt me to say, "Why did God allow this to happen?" Well at my late age, I still needed to learn some things. Once again, most important is not to trust words, especially from an artist at being a liar.

Also, I have learned that since I believe God is real and faithful to His Word, and I daily surrender my life, mind, soul, and body to Him for His care and direction and protection, then I should just trust and praise Him for all I have learned and know about who He is. Also at this time, my car was failing me as well as my health, all serious situations, but day by day my Lord helped me through as He had taught me to trust Him. He also taught me that He is present with me and that I need to stay close to Him so He can use me when that time comes and He will lead me.

We were finishing our afternoon service and I was at the piano putting my things away to take to my car. I stood up to look around the room and caught a glimpse of a lady visiting from another state. My thoughts led me to go welcome her and greet her. When I approached her to let her know how nice it was to see her with us. She smiled and began to tell me about her issues that tore her life apart.

As I listened to her I became aware that her story could have been mine. The Lord had brought me through much the same things many years before and has blessed me with the victory over what I could not do myself. Hers was such a personal story coming to me—a stranger, and by her emotions, I knew the Lord brought us together. Only God can and does choose whom He wants to minister to another. What is the likelihood that anyone would begin to spill their tragedies to a stranger after a greeting? My response to her was, "I understand because the same thing happened to me." She responded with emotional release, and I let her know that God can heal her and help her through. Of course, her burdens were still being carried because of her obvious emotional pain, and I knew the Lord had provided me to help her through. The need for her to have closure was obvious; the burden was so heavy and extremely difficult for her to bear. She needed to know what God had taught me so she could be free.

Everyone was beginning to leave after the service and our time was too short. She was leaving on Thursday so I asked her if she would be coming to the Wednesday night service and that I would like to have time to help her and pray with her. We agreed to be prayer partners on Wednesday. We did and had a bit more time for conversation.

After service on Wednesday, I went to her to say goodbye. Looking right into her eyes, I could see that she was trying to hold back her emotions. I said, "You realize that when you shared so readily with me after we had just met, that it was the Holy Spirit who directed our meeting." She hesitated for a second and with a big emotional smile she said, "Yes, it was." I was able to share with her a bit more before we left. One of her heavy burdens was her children, who were all adults. I knew so because of my experience, so I said to her, "It is going to be very important for you, for victory, as the Lord showed me, you must let your children go." To which she responded tearfully, "I know. He has shown me that, too." We both realized the Lord had appointed our time together. She asked if I had an email, so I provided her with my information with no obligation. She said she would be in touch and if so, I will have the privilege of sharing how God delivered and has kept me. Praise to the Lord who is always able to provide our need as He promised He will, that is if we will ask Him and listen to Him. We need to be available.

Jake Died and Nothing Has Been the Same at Lunch

February 13, 2014

IT WAS WINTERY FEBRUARY AND last month the Lord had opened up a place for me at the senior housing where He had led me. I had been settling in and the lunchroom is one of the few places where I socialized. The difference in life was obvious since I live a conservative lifestyle. I have had few opportunities to witness. Every morning after I wake up, I pray, personalizing Romans 12:1-2, as I place my life into the Lord's hands for His purposes.

At our lunch table, a few of us had become "friends" as we conversed openly about many topics and enjoyed each other's company. I had been asked to play the piano daily for about fifteen to twenty minutes as we settled in for lunch. I played old-time favorites, mixed with western or social and well-known hymns which all seemed to enjoy and it was expected. We had come to enjoy our social time. Three of us, Jake, Donna and I, always sat together and looked forward to the time.

About a year later or so, as we gathered for lunch, Donna came in swearing and yelling loudly, "I wish I knew where I was going when I die!" Well, it was not a good time to deal with that, so I decided to talk to her later sometime about it. Lunch went on as usual. A couple of days later she came in yelling again: "I don't know what kind of a loving God would let you live to eighty-six years old and be almost blind and deaf and cripple." Well, I was near to her at the table and settled and without any forethought immediately out of my mouth came these words, "Perhaps He is allowing you to live, to preserve you from something worse." She looked at me and away a few times as though thinking about what I said, and then out of her mouth came, "You mean hell?!" No more was said, but I knew I must pray and ask the Lord for an opportunity to talk to her because she sounded like she wanted to know.

This happened at the time our friend Jake was ailing and in the hospital. I had just heard that Jake had passed away. It was such a shock, I wanted to go tell Donna and see if she had heard. I knew she would be sad and want to know. When I went to tell her, she invited me in, to her apartment. She truly was shocked by the news. After a short visit, to clear the air it seemed like an appropriate time. I reminded her of her comments about knowing where she was going when she died and began to discuss it with her. I talked about how she could know if she was going to heaven and how she could know that. I presented the way of salvation to her in a warm and friendly way and she listened very intently and quietly. There was not much more said, no response, but I noticed no problem. All seemed well.

Since then, nothing has been the same. It became evident that she was not talking to me at all. Neither was she ever seated next to me at lunch or anywhere else. It was quite clear that she had asked for her seat to be changed. Also since Jake was gone, it did not make a difference, which sheds more light on the situation. Several months later I went down to lunch and the sitting room was empty except for Donna, so I made an effort to talk to her and come to a peaceful place with her. As 1 approached her and asked if there could be some peace between us, before I could say more, her hand shot out at me with these words: "Don't bother, you go your way and I will go mine." So it was clear that this woman who wanted help to know about eternity wanted nothing to do with me after I tried to help her. So I have had to decide to just leave her alone rather get a negative reputation, despite her continual rudeness to me. So I just pass by and don't bother her. How sad to live a life that way, every day letting anger control you with no peace. Thank God she knows the answer to her concerns about eternity and what to do if she ever decides to accept the Lord.

Victory by God Over Evil

June 1, 2014

THE LORD'S POWER WAS SO evident on this special morning that the thrill of His presence and leading overcame me with joy enough to make me shout. It was a usual Sunday morning, and I was getting ready to go to church and watching the time when the need to call my friend to see if she needed a ride was evident to me. She was in her late years with stage-four cancer, gradually losing her sight, and I tried to be available to her needs.

To fully appreciate what the Lord did, I must fill you in on the details. My friend Elaine always made herself available to serve others, and she was always there for Mary, who lived in her senior housing building. Elaine had brought Mary to church for a long time and had tried to help her with her health problems. Her condition was OCD, which involves emotional and behavioral disorders. She is seriously conscious about germs and touching anything someone else may have touched. She often wore plastic gloves, or would avoid handshakes, doorknobs, buttons in elevators; even personal touching of any kind and would cause her to pull herself away.

This morning I finally called Elaine, and she said she was going to pick up a prescription first, so she would not take a ride, and that Mary was not going to church and she may never go again because of things she saw at lunch last week. I hung up the phone and proceeded to get ready to leave by 9:15 as it was already close to 9:00. I made my way downstairs to get to my car, loaded my stuff in and got in to leave for church. When I got to the church, I pulled in being sure to leave Elaine's spot open and I saw her pull in right after I did, but she pulled in farther down the line and others had begun to arrive for Sunday school. I usually had the stuff to take in: my Bible, purse, and lunch for after morning service. I got organized and made it up the steps to the church and down the aisle to get settled. As I made my way halfway down the aisle I looked up and who did I see coming from the other door but Mary. Realizing what a victory that was to overcome, I was so excited that I ran down the aisle to her and hugged her—and she hugged me back!

That was the first time I had ever touched her during the long time we had known each other, even while I was discipling her and other casual times we had been together. She hugged me back! Remembering the issues, I released her and turned back up the aisle to get the things I had dropped on the floor. Then I turned around and hugged her again. The joy over the victory was wonderful to see God working.

After I had talked to Elaine earlier, the Lord led me to call Mary to tell her that she must fight. Knowing that was God's leading I had stopped to make that call. It was already after 9:00 and I did not know if she would answer the phone, but I planned to leave her a message, "to fight." Well, she did answer the phone, to my surprise. I said, "Hello Mary, the Lord has told me to call you and tell you that you are in a war and you must fight." She told me how awful she was feeling and not wanting to go and feeling terrible. I said, "Mary, you can do things you want to do like asking the ladies to make you a cup of coffee when you get to church. If you want to please God, you can choose to go to church. If you do not, then you are choosing to please the Devil instead of listening to and obeying God." Then I prayed for her and I do not even remember what I said. I hung up and went on my way to get to church just a bit after 9:15. Later I found out that she said she only had about two minutes to get dressed and she called Elaine, who had not yet left, and she came to church getting there just a couple of minutes before Sunday school started. Can you imagine what it was like to see her there? All because of the power of God Mary's won over the Devil's efforts to keep her from overcoming her emotions and getting to church. Praise the Lord.

Testimony of Christ's Presence and Power

THIS PARTICULAR FRIDAY WAS SUPPOSED to be a regular day when the family was having its usual get-together for dinner. After eating I tried to get up and out to the kitchen for dessert, and my chair would not slide back, so I gave it a push with my leg, slightly twisting a bit so I could get away from the table. I felt a bit of a stretch, but no real pain or discomfort. Everything seemed normal; we had dessert, visited a bit, and everyone helped put things away and left about four pm.

A couple of hours later I began to feel serious pain in my left knee. It grew worse and soon I could not bend the knee anymore. Using the toilet was very difficult because I could not get up or down without unbearable pain. As time went on, I realized I was not able to bear the pain whether I moved or not. I considered trying to go to bed and waiting to see what morning would bring. I prayed and asked God to show me what to do. It became evident that I was in trouble because I always had to use the bathroom in the middle of the night, and I could not do that without a problem. So I called the ambulance and they came and took me to the emergency room. The doctor there, after consulting with the doctor in charge, said he could not send me home because I could not take care of myself, so they sent me upstairs to be admitted.

Being unable to bend my knee, I spent the next three days using a bedpan until I could be tested and get another evaluation, I was placed in another room where there was another patient, but we never saw each other because the curtain was completely closed around the other patient who remained completely quiet as though there was no one there. We never saw one another or communicated in any way—not a word.

The next day, I discovered a good friend of mine was just down the hall. Her husband happened to see me sitting up as he passed by my door and recognized me. He came in to say hello and, as usual, we had a good discussion about the Lord, the Bible, and how the Lord leads. He offered a prayer for me and left soon after his son and family who were visiting their mother and grandma came in to visit. It was pleasant and we also visited and exchanged conversation about God and His goodness, and His leading in our lives—a regular Christian conversation. After a bit, they also prayed with me and then left to go see their family member. The next day (Sunday) my pastor and his wife came to visit after services at church. It was an enjoyable visit, catching up on health and situations from all parties. As always, the Lord and His goodness were expressed. Before they left, prayer was offered and my Pastor's wife also offered a prayer for my room-mate whom I had not yet met. Later on in the afternoon, a young woman whom I had discipled came in to visit me. She had heard at church that I was in the hospital. We shared about the Lord's work in her life, and she received guidance and counsel as she desired. We both prayed and she left.

Then the unexpected happened. For the first time since I had been in that hospital room, I heard a voice coming through the curtain that had been completely covering the other side of the room. "Patty, I have been so impressed and thrilled by the prayers from your friends and that your pastor's wife prayed for me. Do you think that you could spend some time together with me in prayer tonight before we go to sleep?" What a surprise! I answered, "Of course! We will plan to do that."

I still had not seen her, and she remained quiet through the rest of the time as others came and went. A lady janitor came in and saw me reading my Bible and said, "I need to get a new Bible; someone stole mine." She expounded upon her relationship with God and that she talked with Him all day because He is always with her. We shared and talked about our Christian walk and relationship with the Lord. She left and the time came for my roommate and me to meet face to face and get acquainted. The curtain was opened. After initial greetings, she said, "When I was younger, I asked Jesus to come into my heart and I asked Him to become my Lord and Savior. But I have strayed far and want Him back in my life." We prayed together. She made things right with her Savior and asked Him to forgive her and to "start over."

This was a young girl in her early twenties who had serious health concerns, repeated bouts with pneumonia, damaged organs throughout her body, and a serious smoking problem, which threatens her life. In her young life, she has done just about anything anyone could do while living in this world. She chose to stop smoking to save her life. How she will get back on track with the Lord only she and the Lord know, but I believe she is serious and truthful about doing so. She expressed her thankfulness for our having met and chooses to stay in touch. Before I left the next day, I told her I would bring her a daily devotional full of Bible quotes, and a copy of one of my books for encouragement for her.

The next day, I put on my knee brace and fully intended to take the books to my new friend as early as I could, knowing my energy level, but as much as I tried, I could not get there until evening. As I got into the room, a new roommate asked me who I was looking for. When I told her, she said, "You could not have gotten here at a better time." I went over to the other side and my little friend was having a meltdown, as she called it. Her doctor had just left and the news was not good. I listened and we briefly talked. I gave her the books and put my hand on her shoulder and prayed for her, asking the Lord to have His will for her and to help her in her walk. She interrupted to say to God, "No matter whether I live or die it is OK." She was in His hands. As I left she said she wanted to keep in touch. A short week later, I received a card with a note of thanks and praise to God.

The last information she shared with me in connection with her superior artistic gifts and talents was that her education included special services, for-autistic students.

This explains the extreme silence. Also, who else would be a better roommate for her at this time, but one, like me, who knows the Lord, who has been a teacher of the autistic in a school for the autistic? Isn't God wonderful and powerful to say the least? Our God is great!

> Patty, 3/22/15
>
> I'm finally out of the hospital, got released today on my son's third birthday! My diagnosis remains lung disease more so cystic fibrosis, so I'm still waiting on a lot of test results. Patty, I can't find the words to say thank you from the bottom of my heart. I may be sick, I will remain sick, but with the good Lord back in my life (thanks to you!) and modern medicine, I'll live every day as if it's my last, taking nothing for granted. I love the books you brought to me! You are an incredibly talented writer, and inspiring is an understatement. "His Princess: Love Letters From Your King has kept me as positive as one can be." It's my daily, afternoon, nighttime reminder. If I never met you I don't know if my faith would have become restored. God is good.
>
> I am thinking of your health as well. Hopefully, it is improving daily. Patty, you have changed my life. I wish for you to remain in my life!

> God's spirit shines through in people like you.
>
> "Our people should learn to spend their time doing something useful and worth the whole." Titus 3:14.

As for you, Patty, you've been very much useful. I look up to your knowledge. Hope to hear from you soon. Until then, God Bless.

Testimony of God's Grace for Service

IT WAS TIME TO MAKE a plane trip to California for a family visit. It was better not to leave the week of Christmas, so I got my ticket to leave the sixteenth of December, a Tuesday. I also decided to stay a little bit longer than usual because it may be the last chance I would get to be with the family there. The trip went well and I was greeted by my daughter at the airport without incident. I got settled in at "Grandma's Room" at the kids' lovely home in southern California.

The next day was Wednesday, (AWANA) night, so the evening program was planned and I went along, as usual, to fill in wherever possible to help. Ours was a class of junior-age girls, and I went along to help there. Barbara opened up her class time, gave her story, and then we divided up in groups to work in their books and memorize Scriptures. At that time I was assigned to work with a couple of the girls and to listen to them as they worked to answer their questions and do the memorizing.

I listened to the one who had been here longer and helped her and when she needed no more help, I moved over to the other side of the table to help the other girl; she was trying to learn her verse. I asked her if she understood what the verse was saying about the Holy Spirit. After reading about the Holy Spirit's active presence in our lives, I wanted to be sure she understood what the verse that she was trying to memorize was about. So I explained to her that when we ask Jesus to come into our heart, the Holy Spirit comes in to live in us. When I asked her if she understood, she was unsure. Then I asked if she had accepted Jesus as her Savior; she had not. I offered to help her with that if she was interested in asking Jesus to come into her heart and life. She said that she was, but she wanted her friend to be there with her, which was the first girl I had helped. Because I was new there, I wanted her leader to know what was going on, but she was already pre-occupied, so I was referred to another leader. She took the two girls to a more private and quieter area so they could concentrate and pray. Later, I heard that the girl did accept Christ and then asked if they would let her little brother pray, too. Later I discovered that those children were visitors and I thanked the Lord for the privilege to be involved in their decision for Christ that they had made that night.

God's timing is so special and powerful, and hopefully, something was learned for God's glory. The plane arrangements I had made were such a blessing to have me in a place like that to help someone to come to the Lord. Being a teacher causes me to think that it just makes no sense to try to memorize without understanding the meaning and how it affects you. It is so easy to get caught up in the ritual of what we are doing and we lose the purpose. I hope that all teachers make sure the children understand the words and meanings of what they are doing. Children's souls are precious and can be very sincere without understanding the importance and just trust their teachers. Imagine the privilege—two souls won to Jesus that night. Thank you, Lord!

Naiveté Brings Computer Scam

May 20, 2015

It was a regular day in May, a Saturday evening, and I was viewing family pictures on my computer. The phone rang: "We are servicing your computer and observed you have not updated the services. Your computer has many negatives that need to be fixed." This is the second time this has happened and I ended up having to pay $299 for service. I know very little about computers and this present world, so I listened. Since I had already paid for this kind of service, I thought I may not need it again. I should have learned, but because it sounded legitimate, I decided to listen. Once again I paid for two to three years of service, thinking I really should have help to keep the computer operating. Then a huge change happened.

The service agent began a new line: "Because of the time, Saturday evening, I won't receive the check until Monday and in China that will be too late and I could lose my job." This began to sound strange. He then asked me to write him a check for $2500 and get it to him, and he could then take out the $299 and send the rest of it back to me. This sounded crazy to me that I was to somehow even get my money back. Then I woke up! I told him that there was no way I was going to do that. He persisted, "You will feel very bad and guilty for causing me to lose my job." I strongly refused (should have hung up). Then he said, "You won't enjoy looking through bars at your age." Again I refused to write the large check. He tried once again and I strongly refused and told him to forget it. He then became angry and started shutting down my computer from his end until I was completely shut down.

Since this was Saturday night, I could not get to my bank, but I realized I could do that on Sunday after our second service. Praying as I was going, on Sunday afternoon after our services, somewhere around three pm, I went to my bank. The young man, a supervisor, was wonderful and so helpful. I told him what had happened and he immediately closed my bank account, sent a fax to order new checks for my new account, and we filled out legal forms to report the incident. They had a record of the $299 check I had written. He helped me know everything I had to do. I had to notify Social Security and my teacher retirement to assure my checks would go into my new account. From there, the nightmare started. All the automatic monthly payments that went out from my account, insurances, charge account, electric, and on, all had to be stopped and redirected. All accounts had to be changed as well as my name and address; what a long and trying time. I needed to be sure that no one could get to my new account. Also, my medical coverage had to be changed and Social Security.

It is now been over a month of making all the changes and closing the old accounts. I was feeling so exhausted.

The feelings of insecurity because of all the new accounts and changes had left me feeling drained as well. It was a Tuesday night in June and the phone rang. Since the incident I had just gone through I had not talked to anyone except family and friends. I certainly talked to the Lord and thanked Him for seeing me through and asked Him to help me to be more careful and to lead me and now there was another evening phone call. The information showed me the familiar phone number and I could tell it was from the same organization. I cautiously answered the phone and immediately I noticed a difference. He was American and understandable. He gave me his name and phone number and that he was calling regarding a fraudulent charge of $299 and the check I wrote for service. He was right upfront with me and calmed as I listened. Then I told him what happened and about the manipulation and threats from the calls I received. He apologized for the problem and that the person who talked to me like that would be fired and that he would write me a check to replace the one I wrote and put it in the mail that very night. He asked me if I had the name of the person who did this. I had a couple of names on my list and that seemed to relieve him.

So after that, I just had to wait for the check to see if it was true. I had a new account and was just waiting for all the paperwork, and to get my computer fixed. Thanks to the Lord who came through for me and I learned many things and He gave me the victory! He is so faithful in any circumstances. Praise His name.

Trip To California For The Holiday And Healing

November 25, 2015

A COUPLE OF YEARS AGO, I had moved back to Rhode Island. I had a bout with breast cancer, surgery, and recovery. That seemed to be the beginning of several health issues as I neared the eighty-year-old stage. A few months later another very different and difficult problem hit me with no warning.

It was on a weekday morning and as usual, I woke up to use the bathroom. I rolled over to get out of bed, put my legs over the edge of the bed, planning to stand up, but a huge force threw me back onto the bed and I could not rise. I lay there wondering what happened. I tried again but I could not sit up; a force or power held me down. After several efforts, I reached and grabbed the walker that was usually near the bed. Slowly and with much effort, I managed to stand and get to the phone to call my daughter-in-law for help.

She called the doctor and came to pick me up to get to the doctor. He examined me and I took some tests. He put me on a prescription to help me while waiting for the test results. He could find nothing to indicate a problem. So I used the prescription, and I seemed to come out of it and had no further problem.

Time went on and another spell occurred when I became dizzy and tried to call the kids, but could not get them, so I had to call the ambulance to take me to the ER. After examining me, they diagnosed me with vertigo and watched me there for a while to see the results of the meds they gave me. I was there much of the day, and they decided to release me, but I could not get the kids again. The only other option was to call my church to get someone to take me home. My pastor's wife and their two little boys and her sister came to take me home with my prescription. Again I gradually became stable, but on occasion, a slight imbalance occurred but went away. The time was coming for my trip to California for the holidays, so after some consideration, I decided to go. The doctor could see no major problem, so I got my tickets and prepared to go for Thanksgiving and stay through the holidays after New Years'.

The time came and I got onto the plane—seat number twenty—and settled in. Before long a lady sat next to me and her husband sat next to her, but across the aisle. We visited and the subject of vertigo came up as I shared my experience. She responded, "My husband has dealt with that for years, but there is something you can do to control it. Go to a physical therapist and he will teach you something to help you." She briefly filled me in. When I got to California and my daughter picked me up I told her about what happened. When we got to her house she told her husband and we discussed it a bit. Then each one of them got on the phone to let the family know that I had gotten in and my issue with vertigo. Each of the families had a mother who had experienced the same thing and had a treatment for it. One of them had a video about it, which they sent to us on the computer that very same evening. The next day my daughter and I watched it together, and she said, "Do you want to go for it?" Now she has been a nurse her whole career, so I said, "Sure!" so we did. We followed closely the directions we watched on the video. The first time we did it the one way and it did not seem to do anything, so we tried the other set of directions and after completing the maneuver I sat up and the dizziness was gone! We just looked at each other. She asked me how I felt and I told her that it was gone and we just looked at each other in unbelief. I got up and walked around the bed and it was wonderful—it was gone! Praise the Lord! I was fine—cautious, but fine—the whole rest of the time there. What a wonderful miracle had come!

When I got home I saw a neurologist who referred me to a physical therapist in the same building who then showed me another maneuver to use and I would not have to go see her anymore and she gave me the pictures of the whole maneuver to use if the problem came back. Again, praise the Lord!

When you think of God's intervention by directing my seat on the plane, sitting right next to me with the answers I needed, and family making their calls and all the information getting to me from Rhode Island to California and then completing it in Rhode Island, what a miracle! God is always on the job watching over us. I do not know where the lady on the airplane was coming from or going to, but she had the information to 4111 help me and no one else—not even the doctors I had seen—told me. Praise God! Now I am completely free from the problem and have the maneuver to use if it should ever come back! I have a great Heavenly Father who watches over me.

The Lord Directs My Foot Doctor

April 15, 2016

SINCE CHILDHOOD, I HAVE HAD to wear "special" shoes. There was no serious structural problem, but I remember my mom would take me to Penny's store to get fitted for my shoes. In that day, Penny's had an x-ray machine that I could stand on to see if the shoes I tried on fit me properly. I never had fancy or cute shoes, as we called them then. When I got older, I could wear tennis shoes for playing sports, but for school or church, I wore the soled full shoes with shoelaces. As I aged, I had to have arch supports- depending upon how much money was available for extra things. I was on my feet a lot since I became a classroom schoolteacher and involved in bowling and golf.

As I grew older I had to see foot doctors, and they made specially formed arch supports because of my flat feet and extremely crooked toes. I could get the ugliest foot award. My doctor was excellent. He carefully measured and prepared a mold for me to stand in that formed around every detail for the shape of my foot. Then the mold would go to the lab to be covered with other custom-made layers that were then covered with leather and patches to fit the shape of my feet. They were wonderful but expensive, and my feet never hurt me anymore.

Well, after ten or more years, the molds began to show some wear. For fear that I would lose the support; I decided to go to a foot doctor in Rhode Island where I had recently moved to get some new ones. When I asked my new foot doctor about new inserts, with little concern he just told me that they don't make that kind anymore, but he had some that I could just buy and insert into my shoes; he just needed to know the right size. "What size are your shoes?" he asked, after examining the old support. I told him and he left the room to get them from his supply closet, picked out the nine-and-a-half-wide in a package and unwrapped them and put them in my shoes and that was it. It cost eighty-five dollars, and I got to keep my old inserts.

Well, I wore my shoes with the new inserts, but with much discomfort. I tried to get used to them, but my knees and ankles began to hurt and I was unable to do stairs normally, which became more and more unbearable. After a couple of months, I put my old inserts back in and began to look for a different foot doctor. I did not want to ask my other doctor for a referral, so I did what I should have done in the first place: I went to the Great Physician, my Lord in prayer, and asked Him for directions to find the one I needed and what I should do. I figured the cost may probably be much higher, and my physical problems were becoming a concern. After some trial and error, I found a friend who went regularly to her foot doctor and said that I could go in with her and that he was a nice guy. Also, they did make molds but made out of foam now. So I was able to make an appointment at the same time with her and would also get a ride and learn how to get there. I prayed again, "Lord, please let this doctor be the one I can trust to do what I need for my feet. Please, Lord, I ask you to have the doctor honestly tell me what I should do to solve my foot problem." The appointment time came and he came in very casual and friendly and looked at my inserts and my feet and shoes. He told me that they don't make that kind of insert anymore with the hard plastic mold covered with layers and leather. He said they could make some molds. He looked at my feet again and the inserts. He asked me how old I was and said, "I think I could take these back to my lab and glue the layers of these together and they will last you quite a while. You may not need to get new ones."

So that is what he did. They felt great, the pain in my ankle and knees went away gradually, and my bill was fifty dollars instead of $490, which it would have cost me for new ones that would not have been the same solid quality of my original ones.

That is praise to the Lord for directing that doctor. What doctor would choose from that given his profit except one that was directed by my wonderful Lord, and because I was led to talk to the Lord about it in the first place? The Great Physician led me and directed the doctor to make that decision. Praise the Lord! May we learn to ask the Lord first in all concerns of our lives?

Another Shopping Time with The Lord

JUNE 30, 2016

LAST SEASON WHEN SUMMER WAS over, I decided to throw my old white purse away knowing I would need to get another one the next season. It was worn out. I knew it would be difficult because I wanted one with all the compartments I needed. I also knew I wanted one that was not so wide but still had everything else.

The time had come and on this particular day I had a doctor's appointment, so I thought that on my way home, I would go right over to Ann and Hope Store because it was along the way and I could save some gasoline and some time and energy.

After the stop at the doctor, I went right over to the store and found a close parking spot and got out to go to see what I could find. I soon discovered that Ann and Hope no longer sold clothing and personal items, but only household goods. I was disappointed to have wasted some time and gasoline to go there and not get what I was looking for, but

I am not a shopper and just did not know about that store. I picked up a couple of bath towels I needed, checked out, and started back home. The mall was farther away than I wanted to drive until I got gas on Friday, and I had no idea of other stores in the area without doing a lot of driving, so I decided to just go home when I got to the light. As I approached the light the idea came into my head, "You could find what you want at this store right here." I was right by the Salvation Army store, but I never gave that a thought and the store was right on the way home and less than a mile from my apartment. Well, I trusted the thought as guidance and pulled into the parking lot of the store and found a place right by the door. I had learned that the Lord is always by my side.

The store was busy and I was tired, so I went on my own to see what I could find. I walked a few steps toward the back of the store and just on my left down the next aisle was a stand that held purses. There were one white purse and a few others. It looked pretty new and was the shape I liked, a bit smaller than my old one. I took it down and looked it over; it was like new and with the compartments, I was looking for. It even had a shoulder strap, which would come in handy when I needed to hang on to a banister. It had a green price tag on it: $7.99 Well I probably could not do much better anywhere, and it was in excellent shape, and hardly used by appearances. I took the purse and went over to the checkout stand. The woman at the checkout gave me a serious look and said, "I'm sorry, but the green tag is an error. It is only for the sale of used items. I will have to charge you $8.99 because it is a new purse." I just smiled, thanked her, paid up, and went out to my car. In less than ten minutes, I was in and out of the store with a new white purse exactly like I wanted no parking problems, no waiting in lines, and less than a long city block from my apartment. Praise the Lord! It is everything I wanted in a purse and even cheaper, and the Lord knew right where it was and led me all the way.

Now some people may think me foolish for believing that God bothers Himself with these kinds of things, but my God does. He cares about every need I have and is with me all the time. That is because He sent the Holy Spirit to live inside of me when I asked Jesus to save me many years ago. The Scriptures promise that He will never leave me or forsake me, and that is true and has been my experience. In every place and circumstance, He is always there to meet my every need. Surrender to Him, and He will do the same for you.

Today once again, He proves His presence a couple of months later. I had just ordered some Bible books for my grandchildren and was thanking God for meeting my needs. As I was getting things together I looked over my shoulder to see what I should do next, and on a little stand nearby holding things for me to do, I saw the old white purse that I needed to throw away since I had replaced it with my new one. I hate to throw things away and hesitated to do so. I decided to do just that but decided to pick it up and take another look at it one more time for any rips, etc. In the little pockets where I kept emergency cash, I felt something. When I opened it, I found what I thought was in my new purse: my emergency cash that I had not transferred to my new one. Praise the Lord again. In this aging process, God is protecting me from the forgetfulness. He had prevented me from throwing out the old purse many times I had thought about it as it came into my mind. Oh! Praise the Lord for His watchfulness and love and care!

The Lord Provided A Closet

September 16, 2016

EARLY THIS YEAR THE CLOTH-COVERED closet I had began to just fall apart. After a while, I decided I should get a new one. That would mean to first find one, a way to get it delivered, and the money to pay for it that I had not planned to spend. Because I am not a shopper, I began to ask around to get some suggestions, but without much success. My grandson suggested I get a sturdier one and maybe I should try Bob's Furniture over on Route 2. I knew where the store was generally and put off going there thinking that someday when I was in that neighborhood, I could see what they had. One day I was close to the Lowe's store and went in, but they said they did not have any. I did not know my way around that well, so when I went by Benny's store, I decided to go take a look. Well, they had a black wooden one that was not quite as wide as the other one, and I did need the space for the clothing. Perhaps I could make it work. I had been asking the Lord for direction and help from the beginning; I needed Him to show me what to do, where to go, how much to spend, etc. That one was $79, a bit small, and they do not deliver, so I would have to find a way to get it into my apartment. My kids are usually busy and I hated to bother them, but I thought I could make arrangements as needed. I left Benny's without any commitment.

A couple of weeks later, I got a call from a lady friend who said she was going shopping and said she would look around as she shopped occasionally. She called me a week later to tell me that she went into Lowes and saw one that she thought met the measurements and might be what I was looking for.

She said it cost $199, just what I was looking for, and her description interested me, even though it was a lot more expensive. I thanked her and told her I would look into it. The next day as I was on the way to my kid's house, I left a bit early and planned to pull into Lowes to take a look—not too hopeful because they had told me they did not have any. As I entered the store, the greeting girl met me and asked to help and I told her what I was looking for. She answered that she did not think they had any closets. I told her that a friend had told me she was in there and saw one. Well, she just directed me down an aisle and said that if there were any, I would probably find it down there somewhere in the furnishings department. On the way there, I saw two other employees and asked them. One of them said, "No, we don't have them." But the other girl said, "Sure, come right down this way. Follow me, I'll show you." Sure enough, there it was: a tall, white, closet with shelves or poles for hanging the clothes. I could either buy it in a box to put together, or I could buy the one already standing, but the price would be reduced from $129 to $79 because it was not considered new and was already put together. There were no marks or scratches on it, but I could still have the shelves and as it is. I asked if they delivered and she said they would but only to the door of my apartment building. She suggested that I asked the janitor of our building to bring the dolly out and take it upstairs for me. They would work out a time with us to make that happen. After some thought, I agreed and she made up the order and called for the manager. I was already getting excited and thanking the Lord. When the manager got there, she asked him about the delivery and he said, "If we take it on the flatbed instead of the station wagon, there would be more than one man and they could take it upstairs for you and take it to your room." As this is going on, I am standing there and listening to how the Lord was working this whole thing out with more and more blessings. So we made the arrangements for Tuesday instead of Monday for better timing because Monday is too busy. Of course, she did not know that I had a doctor's appointment on Monday, but my Lord knew.

So, praise the Lord, by His timing, leading and providing in every way, I had a new closet the same size as my old one, that had been reduced to $79 because it was already put together, that would be delivered to my apartment for an additional fee of $65 for delivery all at the same price to my apartment as the smaller one where I could not get it delivered. So what I thought could have cost me over $199, was mine for $144 delivered right to my apartment and room. Besides that, I got it at the store less than a mile from my home, so fewer travel expenses. God had every detail in my favor simply because I asked Him to help me.

One could ask, "Does it pay to include the Lord in any of your needs?" No doubt, He was involved, and I saw blessings galore.

Actions Speak Louder Than Words

October 16, 2016

When I was a child my mom would on occasion say those words. She wanted no pouting, sassing or bawling when we were corrected or punished. To her, that kind of behavior was like correcting or punishing the authority figure and it was not allowed. When there was sadness or disappointment or hurt, it was OK to cry, but there was a time when she would say, "You have cried long enough, now go find something to do." We were not allowed to baby ourselves but learned to accept what we could not change. What she taught us was that she could tell by our actions, the look on our faces, or by the way, we moved around what we were feeling or thinking or how we were emotionally controlled. That certainly is true. Just look at all the actions and behavioral responses that are shown on the TV that have become our teachers.

What does the Scripture tell us about responding to life's problems and disappointments? The book of Proverbs is full of answers about appropriate responses to people, circumstances, trials, losses and other negatives in opposition to how we feel and what we want. It shows how to deal with all the other negatives, sins, losses, and inconveniences. God tells us that He wants us to be an example of how a child of God should behave according to His standards. All through the Bible, and especially in the book of Proverbs, God teaches us and deals with circumstances and tells us how we should endure. He expects us to receive correction His way.

Some Christian leaders have said, "You give me your child for the first seven years of his life, and you can have him." There is much truth in that for young or new parents. I am very much what my parents taught me to be regarding discipline and response to authority. However, I was not saved until I was twenty-one and had gone to college. As a person, I still am pretty much the same as I was in my parents' care regarding authority figures and social problems. Everyone does not have the same kind of temperament or responds to life's problems in the same ways. My parents were from a culture that taught biblical principles, which is much different from many, especially in today's world. The basics were in believing and following biblical teachings and that God is in authority, which goes back to my parents' time and their parents' time.

A basic biblical principle is to witness to others and bring them to a saving knowledge of Jesus Christ. Thus, our behavior should exemplify biblical teachings. Over time people change, problems change, responses change and exemplify the way people have been taught to behave and respond to happiness and strife. This has a lot to do with the way the culture is using the same teachings.

Three and a half years ago I asked the Lord to show me where He wanted me to be, and He led me to the senior housing complex. It certainly is a mission field, but a very pleasant place to live if you don't mind being different. It is a facility for a majority of Jewish and Catholic and other choices of beliefs. It has been a peaceful existence and I have been well accepted by most residents who know me or who have "heard of me." I pretty much stay to myself except for lunchtime, where many of us receive our noon meal. We talk, listen, and joke around, share ideas and generally get to know one another and respect one another. I go to church three times each week, play the piano at lunchtime for a bit, and take care of my life. I play a variety of music including familiar hymns. In the last couple of years as I have aged, I have endured health issues that have made huge changes. Temporarily vertigo affected me, which came and went eventually with the Lord providing all I needed or will need. Then a month ago, as I was on my way walking to my car to go to church, my toes caught the curb and threw me face down into a little hill of dirt with my glasses on. I was bleeding and unable to get up, but God provided a friend and his daughter and another Christian woman, who was also going to church to help. They wiped the blood and dirt off my face and fixed my hair. They helped me up and walked me back into the building and called emergency services. They put a collar on me, took me to the ER where I was until around 1:30 pm. The diagnosis was a broken nose. My glasses were bent and scratched; I had a black eye and bruised forehead, as well as bruises on my face, knees, and legs. I was a mess.

After being home a few days I was not getting any better, so I went to see my family doctor who was very disgusted because no one at the hospital even acknowledged that I had a concussion. So he restricted me to rest and I also needed to wear sunglasses and earplugs to shelter effects of sound and light. So now I was using a walker and had orders of no TV or computer and no driving. So my life was completely changed and restricted to rest, with little freedoms. All I could do was to recover and protect myself as this was happening. The prognosis was three to six months and longer because of my age. Why am I telling you all this?

After a couple of weeks I was sitting down by the door waiting for a ride, and there in the sitting room was a lady, a casual friend, who was sadly waiting for her ride and looking to me off and on. Then she said, "So many things have happened to you recently, and you just keep going on your regular way and coming to lunch." When she finished, the Lord led me to say, "My life belongs to the Lord, and He gives me the strength, grace, and whatever I must have. He watches over me." There was no response, and soon our rides came and we went our separate ways.

This incident caused me to recall another situation when I was coming home from church one time. A couple of women I knew were sitting outside talking and we were all friendly. The one-woman always, since day one, had called me a nun. When I would come into the beauty shop where she was waiting, she always would say, "Oh, here comes the nun." Now she just said it again. Then the other lady who was sitting there, new to the building, said, "Why do you call her a nun because she wears a cross around her neck?" After a few minutes of looking around she answered, "No, it is because of the way she carries herself and conducts her life."

I have never spent any time with this woman personally, but just in and out in passing. Now, discussing people, otherwise known as gossip, is very common here. But that is OK. These things that happen to me and my life in Christ have made it ever so clear that we as Christians have a responsibility to Christ to walk the way He asks us to walk, talks the way He wants us to, and handle our lives as if we know He is with us. It allows praising Him to others. Truly, how many people know who you are and if you belong to Christ? People need to know who helps us through life's hurdles. "Talk is cheap" is another old saying, but when it is obvious by our life that we have something others don't, that witness could lead someone to Christ. The opposite is also true; if people see self-pity or hear cursing, bad-mouth talk, that would drive someone away from Christ if we have at all talked about our Lord. Read the Word, give your life to Christ, and let your life exemplify His teaching. Swearing and taking God's name in vain is too common even among Christians. Something to think about.

A Surprise Blessing

It was a holiday, and I was still reorganizing from my trip during the Christmas holidays. One of my longtime friends who had recently moved into our facility gave me a call. "Hey, can you come up? I need to talk to you."

So I went up there in the early afternoon and she shared some concerns. She is handicapped and going through some physical and other troubles. So we visited a while and it was time for me to go. I said, "I want to pray with you and then I will have to go." So I got up and walked over to her and also invited her aide to join in prayer with us. She willingly came over and we joined hands and prayed. I left and went back to my apartment to continue reorganizing. A couple of days later, my friend called again. She said, "My aide wants to tell you what happened when you were up here the other day." So I went up and this is what happened. The aide looked at me seriously and said, "I was in pain before we prayed the other day, but because of your prayers, my pain completely went away." What a blessing. Praise the Lord!

I did share praise with her to the Lord, but I told her that the Lord is faithful to all who call on Him, and the only part I had in her relief from pain was that I prayed to Him and because she was there too, He chose to free her from pain, too, and He was the one who did the healing. We all can have that same relationship with him if we go to Him and ask. This is just another example of the Lord's presence when we have a relationship with Him. Praise to the Lord.

Jesus Leads Anytime All the Time

FOR THE PAST MONTHS AND days I had been thinking off and on about singing again at church. Our pastor has been here just a bit over a year and all of our programs are not fully established yet, so there is no schedule and I have not wanted to push in with so much they have on their schedule. But someone had asked me a while back to sing a song that has a good message that I had sung before. As I thought and prayed about it, another song came to my mind–off and on there it was again, "Follow Me." One day I even looked through my music folder to see if I had a copy of the music, and sure enough, I did. I even had made an extra copy.

Sometimes, in the middle of the night, the song would play through my mind, and again I would think that I should sing that song. I believe that all our service should be in His time, will, and place. I also wanted to think of a verse to go along as a testimony with the message in the song. So I practiced on occasion during the day, time and again just to stay familiar with the tune and words. I don't own a piano, so just as I am doing my work, I would go over the words and think, "I need to sing that song at church sometime. I wonder what verse I should use with it." Time went on—holidays, recovery from a fall and concussion, more holidays, and catching up. I would also think about a Scripture verse I could use with it. Then one night as I lay sleeping I recalled the words of the song, "Follow Me" and a few of the lyrics, and then I continued sleeping.

This morning I got up a bit later than usual, had a prayer to start my day, as usual, washed up, got dressed and made my breakfast. The first thing after the basics, I have my devotional time. The last part of my devotions is to read a chapter in the New Testament. I had been in the Gospel of John and today was the last chapter. I have read that book many times, but today, for the first time I realized that chapter is about time with His disciples after Jesus had risen from the dead. This was the third time He had met with them face to face since His crucifixion. He had risen from the dead and chosen to meet with them with His special message before He went back to heaven. He talked to them about service for Him. Three different times He asked one of the three disciples the same thing: "Do you love me?" They each gave a positive response individually to the question, "Do you love me?" They all gave the same response, "Yes, I love you." Then He said, "If you love me, follow me"—there was the scripture I was looking for to use with my song-"Follow Me."

After that happening, I chose to pursue the opportunity to share that message, having been provided with the scripture I was looking for, right from the Savior himself. Praise the Lord!

The Lord Knew—I Did Not

Psalm 37:3-7

SINCE I RETURNED FROM VISITING family over the holidays, I had a lot of catching up to do—piles of mail, putting things away, etc. I had also been recovering from a concussion from a few months ago and life had been a challenge. I am learning that since I am in my 80s, I need to slow down.

Winter was showing itself with snow on the ground off and on, and I had not driven since September, three months before, so I was relearning to a degree. It is not easy for me to bother anyone to help me take care of things. One of those things was that the shoes that I wear for winter months, plus those I had been wearing, both needed to have new taps on the heels. The shoes I need to wear are expensive and were fairly new. I had been asking around to see if anyone knew of a shoe repair shop close by, called "cobblers" around here. I knew of a couple, but for one reason or another, it was not easy to get there for service. I was concerned that I would wear them out before I could get them fixed. Day by day my concerns grew worse, and I wanted to get them fixed so I could move on to my next project.

Finally, I discovered another store, but when I went online for directions there were notices of it being closed for illness. I was told they had reopened. I sought the Lord again for guidance to help me make a decision or find a place. One day a couple said they knew of a couple of places, and that they would help me find them. The closest one had closed! We did find another one in an area close to me. It was easy to get to and even had a parking lot; however, since it was a legal holiday, it was presently closed, so I went back home without my shoes fixed.

The next problem was with the weather. First, several inches of snow fell and my car was covered. By the next week, freezing rain, and then sunshine. I decided to either get a hold of the store by phone to see if they were available, or to just take my shoes to the other place, leave them, and make an extra trip and pick them up later. The next day I gave the store a call late morning and, sure enough, they answered the phone; they were open. I got an appointment for 1:30, so I would leave right after lunch. It had begun to drizzle a bit, but no problem. I got into my car and since it was drizzling I turned on my wipers. To my shock, the wipers made a horrible noise and crossed each other in the middle of the windshield. All along I had been praying about this situation, and now another decision. Instead of surrendering to my fears, I believed I should continue on my way to the store, trusting the Lord, thinking I could be careful and stop at the gas station on the way and get the wipers fixed. I brushed the window free from water and carefully drove to the gas station, but found out that all they did was pump gas. Then I remembered that just up the road was the place where I usually took my car for service. So I cleared my windshield again and soon I pulled in and went in to see if I could get some help. They were not busy so I said, "I am in kind of an emergency." I have an appointment at 1:30, and my wipers are broken. One of the workers got right to it, pulled my car in, and soon came out showing me the wipers but said, "The wipers are broken, but everything else is OK." He came back in a few minutes and said, "You are all set. Just charge her for the wipers, not the services." Soon I was back on the road to find the shoe store, and before long there it was: Shoe Repair. I pulled in at 1:32. Praise the Lord! What a relief!

I grabbed my shoe bag out of the back seat and went in. The man was just finishing up on a shoe. We talked a bit as he worked on my shoes, and he began to talk about the election. "I'm a Christian, born again in 1969, and I can't wait until this is over," I responded by telling him that I also am a Christian, since 1955. He continued the conversation. Then he told me that his store was not open all the time because of his health—he has cancer. We chatted a bit and when he had finished the shoes, he told me how much I owed, and then he said, "I'm going to come and give you a big hug." And he did.

Finally, my shoes were fixed. Praise the Lord. The Lord knew my wipers needed to be fixed, too. He also knew I would know they needed to be fixed if I had to use them. He knew I would have to get them fixed. He knew all the details that I would have to deal with soon. So in His perfect time, I was able to get both needs met and I would discover the need because of the rain. Both issues were cared for on time and in less than an hour in one trip. I only knew a part of the plan. The Lord knew all the details and what I would need to take care of all of them in less than an hour and even less expensive with no extra inconvenience. Praise the Lord! It is so great to belong to the Lord! I did not need to get frustrated over the issue with my shoes because the Lord knew my need. Thank you, Jesus.

And besides that, I met another Christian person who witnessed to me, I found a good shoe repair store, and God has been glorified.

Call and I Will Answer

March 2017

WHAT A WONDERFUL WAY TO end this writing: a prayer-answering God. A few days ago, my printer shot forth a message that I was low on ink and I was getting close to the end of my writing. I had hoped the ink would last until I was finished and then I could buy more ink when I got my new charge card. The other one I had to throw away because of a scam call I received the day before. Also, at my age, I do not drive more than I have to for grocery shopping, etc. Also, I wanted to complete my writing so I would not lose part of it or forget where I stopped. Anyway, I was finishing that writing and got it done hoping the ink would last. I always make two copies of all the stories I write, and this one had two pages. When I printed the story, one whole copy was complete the second copy was on the way near the end of the second page and then "Out of Ink". What a blessing; I had all I needed for the whole main copy. I really could wait to get more ink until I got a new charge card, which was to be coming in seven to ten days. I could then have all my pages in the right place. Praise to the Lord!

I was planning to get by from doing any shopping until I got the new card because that helps me to keep track of where I spent the money. So the days went by, and I was down to the place of needing to get some things, and I unexpectedly received a check in the mail from the eye doctor, I had overpaid for services. So then I could cash that and manage. On Monday, I was on my way to go to the bank to cash the check and I unexpectedly met a lady in the hall where I live. She helped me to take the ink holder out of my printer and said she would help me put a new one back in when I was able to buy more. She then said, "I am going to Wal-Mart, would you like for me to pick up some ink for you while I am there and you can pay me when I get back?" So I thankfully agreed to decide that by then I would use the check money for that, hoping the card would soon come in the mail. So I went to the bank, got the check cashed, and went back to my room to wait until she came with the ink. Well, she did not go to Wal-Mart until later in the afternoon and, praise the Lord, when the mail came, the new charge card was there right on time. So I had the cash and I could pay her, and I had the card so I was able to do the grocery shopping and get the gasoline that I had been waiting to buy on my next trip to town. No need to stress or worry, because God has everything in control as we trust Him to do for us. Praise my wonderful Lord!

Epilogue

January 2, 2017

Every Christian must understand that our relationship with Jesus Christ includes the presence, benefits, and power of the Holy Spirit who comes in when we die to ourselves and invite Him into our lives. The gospel of John tells us in chapters 14-16 that the Holy Spirit comes into lives because Jesus went up to heaven and He sent the Holy Spirit to live in us and teach us all things. Read those chapters for a complete understanding and details of what you have when you accept Jesus as Savior. We must die to ourselves and receive the benefits that God gave us when He sent the Holy Spirit to teach us all things.

When God made us, He equipped us with talents and abilities to use as we live this life after accepting Christ. He had a plan, as He says in Jeremiah 1:5, "Before I formed you in the womb I knew you." We have an enemy who will do all he can to destroy the work of the LORD in us (John 14:30, II Corinthians 2:11, and Ephesians 4:27). The Scriptures say what Satan is trying to gain. This is spiritual warfare—direct and indirect attacks against us. The Holy Spirit protects all believers when we allow Him to direct us. He will not force us to follow Him: we either live for the Lord or ourselves. Satan uses passivity and deception if we try to live two lives.

The Holy Spirit's ministry in us is experienced in different ways. It can be spontaneous, planned, or He can give insights or understanding. He can comfort, encourage, or give strength in a variety of situations and personal matters. He helps us to use the gifts God has given us. We are channels for the Spirit to use to do God's work. He can reveal God's truths and meaningful input. Living in the Spirit helps us build up and edify each other as we share and experience the power of His presence. As we learn more about how the Spirit works, it will give opportunities to reveal and share God's presence, power, and victory. Hopefully, by reading this information you will be sharing and claiming your victories as you exercise your spiritual weapons, which will greatly open doors for witnessing. Also, your answered prayers and guidance will be an acknowledgment of your prayer and relationship with and through the Lord Jesus Christ.

Some of these writings may seem repetitious, but these truths are so important they must be emphasized because it is rare to hear anyone talking about the Holy Spirit, and it is such a blessed way of life.

Resources and References

Daily Morning Contact with My Lord

Heavenly Father, in the name of Jesus I come to you and ask you to forgive me of all my sins of thought, word, or deed. Cleanse me of sinful thoughts and attitudes, in the name of Jesus. I choose to submit to your authority in all areas of my life for your glory and service to you.

Father, I present my body, mind, and spirit as a living sacrifice, holy and acceptable to you by the blood of Jesus. I choose not to be conformed to this world, but to be transformed by the renewing of my mind, that I may prove that which is good and acceptable in your sight.

May the words of my mouth and the thoughts and ideas of my mind and heart be acceptable in your sight so that I may perform that which is pleasing to You.

Lord, teach me to number my days and apply my heart to wisdom, so I may complete the work and plan you have for me to do. Father, be present and work in me to do what you want in thought, word, and deed. Fill me with Your Spirit, that I may fulfill your purpose for me.

As I go through this day, please make the pathway clear before me, so that I might complete what you have for me to do. Keep me safe and free from attacks and interference from the Devil as I move about in the place in life where you have brought me, as well as in the world around me. I need You, Father, and thank You for sending Jesus to die for me. Amen.

This is not memorized and can be personalized to each individual, but the areas covered are important to consider. For my Bible studies, I read one chapter each in the Old Testament, Psalms, Proverbs, and New Testament daily beginning in chapter one every month in the Proverbs and Psalms. The plan is to read through the Bible from Genesis to Revelation, and to read through the Psalms and start again and to read through the Proverbs each month using a plan that works best for each individual. Believe me; it will never get boring because you continue to learn new information built upon what you have already learned. I have been doing this since 1980, where I was first taught to read my Bible daily.

The plan for my life has been based upon these verses for direction.

Romans 12:1; 2 Matthew 6:33; Jeremiah 1:5
God Bless You

Deuteronomy: Listen To God

Deuteronomy is one of my favorite books of the Bible; it is so personal and direct from God to man. It gives us specific directions and experiences of a man with God. To motivate a bit, the references below will provide basic insights about the relationship He wants with us. Hopefully, the portions of Scriptures below will motivate the reader to look them up and perhaps read the wonderful information that is so relevant to all of us. Enjoy!

"You shall love the LORD and always keep His charge, statutes, ordinances and His commandments" (Deuteronomy 11:1).

13: "His promises will come about IF you listen obediently to His commandments" (which He explains).

16: "Beware that your heart is not deceived and then turned away to serve and worship other gods." (Read the results)

18: "Impress these instructions on your heart and soul so your life will be an example of His teaching." (Body language)

19: "Teach them to your children in every walk of life."

20: Your household should live an example of the teachings and bear the reputation of the same.

22: "Keep all His teachings, to love Him, walk in His ways, hold fast to Him and He will be your provider and protector."

26: All He has written, "I have set before you a blessing and a curse." IF you listen, a blessing; IF you don't, a curse. "Be careful to do all the statutes and judgments there."

These wonderful and powerful words from the Lord God, He wrote to His people as they were about to go across the Jordon to the Promised Land. All of us are on our journey; we either have a religion or a relationship. The same words are written to us again and again throughout the Scriptures.

7: "My son, keep my words… and my commandments and live… and my teachings as the apple of your eye and bind them upon your fingers… write them on your heart."

Hopefully, you will be encouraged to fully read these references and to be able to enjoy all the blessings our God has for you, and may your relationship with the Lord be as precious as it really can be.

Ask and you shall receive, Amen!

Helpful Verses: Presence of the Holy Spirit

From Genesis through Revelation the Scriptures give examples of who the Holy Spirit is, how He operates, and how He works in our lives. A Christian must have basic wisdom and understanding about the power of the Holy Spirit, but the subject is grossly ignored by religion in today's world. Since this book is about becoming familiar with these truths, I have included here some specific scriptures to help you to get started.

The stories that are shared in the book are examples of His power, leading, and presence to help you become aware and to acknowledge His expression and work in your life. First, understand that the Holy Spirit's presence will be in anyone who has asked Jesus to forgive his sin and to become his Savior and to come into his life. The words you use are individual, but God knows your heart and will respond accordingly. This topic is not discussed, largely because it is so easy to get involved in prayer, Bible study, and church activities, which are necessary for growth. If the subject is not taught how to live and trust this unseen Person in our lives, He becomes ignored and forgotten as our source of power for our daily walk. I hope that this writing will bring many blessings into your life because you may learn what you have by experiencing the presence of the Holy Spirit as your best friend.

The following verses should increase your present understandings about the Holy Spirit function in your Christian life, basically by asking Him to be involved in whatever you are doing or the choices you make.

I Corinthians 1:12-14; 2:12, 13-14,15,16
II Corinthians 2:11; 5:16-17
Colossians 1:28; 3:5
Galatians 3:1-14
Ephesians 2:1-2; 4:1-27; 5:15-21; 6:10-13
Isaiah 65:24
James 4:7
Jeremiah 1:5
John 1:14-16; 7:37-39; 14:13-14; 16:26-27
I John 3:8
Luke 12:8-12; 11:13
Matthew 3:5-6;12:32-33

Proverbs 3:5-6; 15:2, 3; 25:11-12
I Peter 4:10-11; 5:8-10
Romans 6:1-2; 8; 15; 12:1-2

Proverbs 1:1-7

Proverbs provide wisdom for living today with expectations for what our life should exemplify as we live for the Lord.

1: To produce the skill of Godly living by wisdom through receiving instruction and discernment.

2: To know instruction and sayings of understanding.

3: To receive instruction in wise behavior, righteousness, justice, and equity.

4: To give prudence to the naive and knowledge and discretion to the youth.

5: To hear and increase learning, receive counsel to understand 6: "Fear of the Lord is the beginning of wisdom."

"Fools despise wisdom and instruction."

The book of Proverbs can give anyone the information they need to handle any issue that may happen in a lifetime. Read it daily each month, and then start again and it will guide you as you go through your life and will never seem repetitious.

Scriptural Wisdom and Warnings

Galatians 5:1 says, "It was for freedom that Christ set you free." Jesus encourages us to "continue in His Word and you will know the truth and the truth will set you free" (John 8:31-32).

We must understand that Satan is the great deceiver, and everything God gives us opens a door for our enemy who will either mislead us, try to confuse us, and/or provide some way to lead us astray to get on the wrong track. This writing is a serious attempt to develop the interest and desire to draw closer to our God and to understand that Jesus sent us a helper, the Holy Spirit, to be with us and to live in us so that we may continue the work He initially came to do: to understand that Jesus wants everyone to accept Him as their personal Savior and spend eternity with Him. We should share these truths with others so they can be saved and to continue the work. Unfortunately, during my lifetime the Holy Spirit has not been talked about as an important part of my life that He is intended to be, and that is why I am taking the responsibility to help change that. He is the power we have in us IF we have accepted Jesus as our Savior. I pray that the message will be made plain through this writing. It is made very clear in the gospel of John chapters 14-16 and many other references.

This being true, we must understand that Satan will do all he can to turn people away from the truth and cause them to go to hell. He has provided our world with many opposing religious beliefs and works, such as the occults and other evil spirit practices, and even magic and using our birthdays and handwriting, all under the guise of entertainment or testing our curiosity. These are all distractions about the spirit world to turn us away from the truth and reality of the Holy Spirit. All of these practices are forbidden in Scripture, some of which I will provide here.

Satan is real and fights against any teaching of the one and only True God—the Creator of heaven and earth. This war started in the garden at the creation. Be aware, the enemy does not want this writing to be seen or accepted. So there are evil spirits at work everywhere against the Holy Spirit. Do be in prayer, and surrender your heart, soul, mind, and body to the Lord God so you will be able to receive the truths about the Holy Spirit from Jesus Christ. You need Him so you can spend eternity with Him, and so He can enrich your life as long as you are alive here on earth.

Following are the Bible references about occult-type activity and beliefs so you can be aware and free from the oppression of Satan so you will have victory as you live for Jesus. Exodus 20:3-5 tells us, "You shall have no other Gods before me."

Exodus 22:18
Deuteronomy 18:9-12

Leviticus 19:26; 31; 20:6; 27
I Chronicles 10:13-14
Isaiah 8:19
Jeremiah 27:9-10
Zechariah 10:2
Malachi3:5 Acts 16:16-18; 19:19
Galatians 5:16
Revelation 21:8; 22:14, 15

"Occult involvement breaks the first commandment and invokes God's curse" (Exodus 20:3-5).

One Last Exhortation

It is extremely important for you to know and understand that when you truly and seriously surrender your life to the Lord Jesus Christ, that you will have an enemy—an evil spirit, the Devil—who will try to discourage you and prevent you from growing and staying close to the Lord. Your life will change in ways you may not even think about or recognize. You must continue in your daily Bible reading and prayer, and learn and live what the Bible teaches. You will develop your relationship with the Lord through the presence of the Holy Spirit who is in you. The reading and praying will help you to know how to live, so the Devil cannot defeat you. Pray against temptation and sinful choices. Satan will try to take advantage of you, so do not be ignorant of his ways. Below are scriptures that will help you to resist the temptations. First Peter 5:8 warns, "Be of sober spirit, be on the alert. The adversary the devil prowls around like a roaring lion seeking whom he may devour." You may not see him because he is an evil spirit, or maybe working through an unsaved acquaintance. He will even disguise himself as an "angel of light" (II Corinthians 11:14). In this world, the Devil has forces of darkness and spiritual wickedness that you may not see.

Read the following verses, stay close to the Lord. Beware and be blessed!

II Corinthians 2:11; 11:14
Ephesians 4:14; 6:10, 11,12
James 4:7
John 10:10
I John 3:6-8-9
I Peter 5:6, 7, 8

www.ingramcontent.com/pod-product-compliance
Ingram Content Group UK Ltd.
Pitfield, Milton Keynes, MK11 3LW, UK
UKHW041820200726
13854UKWH00001BA/139